God Made Me Most Wonderfully

L.J. SATTGAST
ILLUSTRATED BY JULIE PARK

To the parent—
These poems were inspired by
Psalm 139: 14—"I will praise you because I
am fearfully and wonderfully made." May
they be the start of many lively and
interesting conversations about the
wonderful bodies God has given us!
LJS

Chariot Books
David C. Cook Publishing Co.

I can take my bucket
  and fill it up with sand,
Turn it upside down
  and build a castle with my hands.

But only God can paint the sky
  and make the land and seas,
And fill the world with animals
  and lovely plants and trees.

I can take a crayon
  and draw a little girl,
Give her eyes and nose and mouth
  and hair that likes to curl.

But only God could ever make
  a boy or girl like me,
Who plays with sand and loves to build
  a castle by the sea.

The flowers need to breath the air
Just like me.
The monkeys at the zoo can stare
Just like me.
But no one else has just my eyes
Or color of my hair,
There's no one else in all the world
Just like me.

Eyes are for . . .
Seeing airplanes in the sky,
Watching ants go marching by,
Chasing butterflies in the park,
Falling asleep after dark.

Eyes are for . . .
Playing games like hide and seek,
Making sure you never peek.
How many children do *you* see
Trying hard to hide from me?

After dark, when all is still,
I creep up to my windowsill
And listen to the quiet sound
Of crickets chirping on the ground.

All day long I hear the noise
Of barking dogs and shouting boys,
Cars that honk and trucks that roar,
The slamming of the kitchen door.

But when my bedtime comes around
I listen to the quiet sounds . . .
Like crickets chirping on the ground.

With my nose
I sniff a rose
So delicate and sweet,
But better if
I get a whiff
Of something good to eat!

"That pie smells nice—
I'd like a slice,
It really wouldn't hurt . . . "
Mom shook her head,
And then she said
"You'll have some for dessert!"

Katie likes to kiss her friends,
Tommy talks awhile.
Cindy bursts out laughing,
And Andrew loves to smile.

Amy wants to whisper,
Sally's going to pout.
Brian tries to sing a song,
But Lewis starts to shout.

We can talk or laugh or sing,
Whisper, smile or shout,
We can do so many things
With just one little mouth.

Blow, wind, blow.
I can blow too . . .
Dandelion seeds go up in the air,
Floating away to who knows where.
Wherever they land new flowers will grow
And make more dandelions for children to blow.

Blow, wind, blow.
I can blow too . . .
Silvery bubbles in my bath,
Shining and shimmering, making me laugh!
Sailing up in the air and then
Floating back down to my bathtub again.
POP!

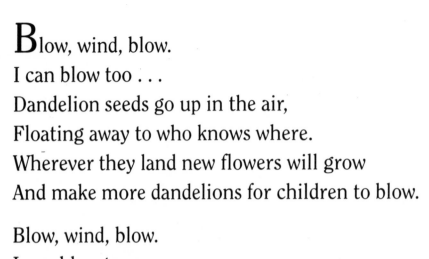

I take a bite
and chew it up,
I drink some water
from my cup,
I swallow hard
and down it goes,
Does it fall down
into my toes?

No! No!
It goes into my tummy,
All the food
that tastes so yummy!
It makes me grow up
big and strong,
And helps me play
the whole day long.

When's a good time to hug?

Early in the morning
When the sun is bright,
I throw my arms around you
And start the day out right.

Later on at snack time
I'm ready for some food.
Along with milk and cookies
A hug can sure feel good.

When I ride my tricycle
I sometimes fall off twice.
I cry, and crawl into your lap—
A hug can be so nice!

After bedtime stories
And turning out the light,
Just before I fall asleep
I hug and kiss good night.

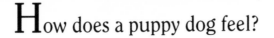

How does a puppy dog feel?

With my fingers I can tell
His nose is cold and wet,
He has the softest furry coat
Of anyone I've met.

A tail that wags from side to side
And ears as smooth as silk,
He licks me with his warm wet tongue
And begs to share my milk.

I feel his teeth so sharp and small
When he pretends to bite,
O puppy dog! Won't you hold still
And let me hug you tight!

Look at me! I'm on my bike—
Pedaling fast is what I like!
My strong legs go up and down,
And the wheels of my bike
Go round and round.

Here I come, I'm rolling fast—
Watch as I go zooming past!
I'll go to the end of the block and then
I'll come right back
And do it again!

My knees that bend and move all day
Are quiet when it's time to pray.
"Bless mom and dad and sister too,
And don't forget, God—I love You!"

Do you suppose
I have ten toes
So I can make them wiggle?
Or so someone
Can tickle them
And make me laugh and giggle!

Who can jump up in the air?
Who can hop from stair to stair?
Make a tower out of blocks,
Fill a pocket full of rocks?

Who can watch a bumble bee?
Who can sing a melody?
Eat some popcorn at the zoo,
Play a game of peek-a-boo?

Who can do it? Here's a clue—
It's someone sitting close to you.
I can do it! Can't you see?
God made me most wonderfully!